E-COMMERCE WEB DESIGN UNLOCKED

The Practical Guide to Building a High-Converting Online Store

Danielle Mead

CONTENTS

Title Page

Copyright

Why Web Design Matters in E-Commerce   1

Understanding User Experience (UX) for Online   9
Stores

Homepage Design & Layout   18

How to Create Effective Landing Pages That   28
Convert

Product Page Optimization   32

Checkout Process & Cart Abandonment   45
Reduction

Designing for SEO and Accessibility   52

Leveraging Apps & Plugins Without   62
Overloading Your Site

Conclusion: Bringing It All Together   68

About The Author   75

WHY WEB DESIGN MATTERS IN E-COMMERCE

When you think about what makes an online store successful, web design might not be the first thing that comes to mind. But in reality, it's one of the most critical factors influencing whether a visitor becomes a paying customer. Your website isn't just a digital storefront – it's the first impression your business makes on potential buyers. If a site looks outdated, cluttered, or difficult to navigate, customers will likely leave within seconds. You've probably had that experience yourself while shopping online. A confusing or unattractive website doesn't inspire trust, and without trust, people won't feel comfortable making a purchase.

A well-designed online store, on the other hand, immediately reassures visitors that they're in the right place. The layout should be intuitive, guiding customers seamlessly from the homepage to product pages and, ultimately, to checkout. Every design decision – from the size of your images to the placement of your navigation menu – affects how easy it is for shoppers to browse, find what they need, and complete their purchase. If there's any friction along the way, whether it's a slow-loading page or a cluttered interface, customers may decide it's not worth the effort and leave for a competitor's site.

Strong web design also plays a vital role in building credibility. Think about how color choices, fonts, and overall aesthetics shape the perception of a brand. A cohesive, professional-looking site signals reliability, while an inconsistent or unpolished design can make even a legitimate business look untrustworthy. Familiarity is another key component – customers feel more comfortable when a website follows expected design patterns. For example, placing the shopping cart in the top right corner or ensuring your checkout button is easy to find helps create a smooth, intuitive experience.

Beyond influencing customer behavior, your website's design directly impacts search engine optimization (SEO). Google and other search engines prioritize factors like page speed, mobile responsiveness, and structured navigation when ranking sites. A slow, poorly optimized site won't just turn customers away – it will also be harder to find in search results, meaning you'll lose out on valuable organic traffic. By prioritizing a fast, mobile-friendly design with clear navigation, you're not just enhancing user experience; you're also boosting your store's visibility and sales potential.

The Role of SaaS Platforms (Shopify, BigCommerce, WooCommerce, etc.)

For most online store owners, building a website from scratch isn't practical. That's where SaaS (Software as a Service) platforms like Shopify, BigCommerce, and WooCommerce come in. These platforms provide ready-made frameworks that make it easy to set up and manage an online store without needing advanced technical skills.

Each platform has its strengths, and choosing the right one depends on your business goals. Shopify is one of the most popular options, particularly for beginners. It's known for its user-friendly interface, robust app marketplace, and seamless integrations. If you're looking for an easy, plug-and-play solution that allows you to start selling quickly, Shopify is a great choice. BigCommerce, on the other hand, is ideal for businesses that require more built-in functionality and scalability. Unlike Shopify, which often requires third-party apps to extend its features, BigCommerce includes a wide range of advanced tools right out of the box, making it a strong option for larger businesses, B2B companies or those planning for rapid growth. WooCommerce is another powerful choice, especially if you're already using WordPress. As a plugin rather than a standalone platform, WooCommerce offers a lot of flexibility, giving you complete control over your store's design, features, and functionality. If you're comfortable with a more hands-on approach and want maximum customization, WooCommerce may be the best fit.

Customizing Your Store Without Code

One of the best things about modern e-commerce platforms is that you don't need to be a developer to create a beautifully designed store. Many SaaS platforms come with intuitive drag-and-drop editors that make customization simple. Shopify's Theme Editor, for instance, allows you to modify colors, fonts, layouts, and even homepage sections with just a few clicks. BigCommerce offers a similar feature called Page Builder, which lets you visually edit your store's design without ever touching a line of code.

Choosing the right theme is one of the easiest ways to ensure your store looks polished and professional. Most platforms offer a wide selection of free and paid themes designed to work seamlessly with their system. While it can be tempting to opt for a flashy, unique design, I always recommend prioritizing usability and responsiveness. A clean, well-structured theme that aligns with your brand will perform better in the long run than a complicated design that confuses customers.

Even small tweaks – like adjusting your button colors to match your brand or ensuring your fonts are legible on all devices – can make a big difference in how professional and trustworthy your store appears. When done right, these simple, no-code changes can help you build a site that feels uniquely yours without requiring a developer.

Advanced Customization For Developers

For those who want even more control over their store's design and functionality, most SaaS platforms also support custom coding. Shopify, BigCommerce, and WooCommerce all allow developers to modify HTML, CSS, and JavaScript, enabling deeper customization beyond what's possible with built-in tools.

If your business has specific branding requirements or needs unique functionality, working with a developer to make these changes can be a worthwhile investment. WooCommerce, in particular, is an excellent choice for store owners who want maximum flexibility. Since it runs on WordPress, it integrates with thousands of plugins and themes, making it one of the most customizable e-commerce solutions available.

No matter which platform you choose, the key is to balance customization with usability. Overcomplicating your site with excessive modifications can sometimes do more harm than good. The best online stores keep their design clean, their navigation intuitive, and their customer experience seamless, whether they're built with no-code tools or custom development.

By leveraging the power of SaaS platforms, you can focus on what really matters – growing your business – while letting the platform handle the technical heavy lifting. Whether you want a quick and easy setup or a fully customized storefront, today's e-commerce solutions offer the flexibility you need to create a store that works for your business.

Common Web Design Mistakes Store Owners Make

Even with all these tools available, many store owners make design choices that unintentionally hurt the user experience. Here are some of the most common mistakes I see store owners making and how to avoid them.

Logo Too Large

Many store owners believe that having a large logo makes their brand more recognizable, but oversized logos can push down important content, forcing users to scroll unnecessarily before accessing products. The best practice is to keep your logo proportional – typically no more than 15% of the screen height – so that the navigation menu, search bar, and cart icon remain easily accessible.

Excessive Use Of Colors

While using brand colors is important, going overboard with too many contrasting hues can create a chaotic, unprofessional look. Stick to two or three main colors that complement each other.

For example, a clean and modern store might use a white background with black text and a bold accent color for buttons. Good design is about balance – your color scheme should enhance readability, not distract from it.

A poor color scheme can also impact readability. Neon colors or clashing hues can strain the eyes, while overly dark backgrounds with light text can be difficult to read.

Poor Text Contrast

Readability is key, and one of the most common mistakes I see is using text colors that don't contrast well with the background. Light gray text on a white background or red text on black can be difficult to read, frustrating visitors. Following accessibility guidelines – such as maintaining a contrast ratio of at least 4.5:1 for body text – ensures your site is easy on the eyes.

Small Font Sizes

Text that is too small makes it difficult for customers to read product descriptions or important information. A good rule of thumb is to keep body text at a minimum of 14px or 15px and ensure that headings are bold and distinct. Larger font sizes improve readability, especially on mobile devices where screens are smaller.

Buttons Too Small To Click On Mobile Devices

With more people shopping on mobile, your store's design must be mobile-friendly. Small buttons that are difficult to tap can frustrate users and lead to abandoned carts. The best practice is to make buttons at least 48px wide, or ideally full screen width, so that they're easy to click on touchscreens.

Overly Complex Category Menus

While dropdown menus help organize large inventories, overly complex category menus can be difficult to navigate. If category lists wrap onto multiple lines or contain too many subcategories, customers may struggle to find the right products. Try to limit main categories to 5-7 items, using subcategories sparingly.

Moving Elements That Disrupt User Experience

Some websites include sticky menus, hover effects, or auto-sliding banners that move unpredictably. While these features may seem engaging, they can create usability problems. For example, a menu that shifts on hover can cause accidental clicks, disrupting navigation.

Animations and effects should enhance – not hinder – the shopping experience. If using movement, it should be subtle and purposeful, not distracting to customers focused on finding products and completing purchases.

UNDERSTANDING USER EXPERIENCE (UX) FOR ONLINE STORES

The Importance of Simplicity and Intuitive Navigation

One of the biggest challenges in e-commerce is keeping shoppers engaged long enough to turn them into paying customers. A confusing or cluttered website can quickly drive potential buyers away, while a well-organized, intuitive shopping experience encourages them to browse, explore, and complete their purchases. I've seen countless online stores struggle simply because their navigation is too complex or overwhelming. That's why prioritizing simplicity and clarity in your site's layout is critical to your success.

The goal is to create a seamless experience where shoppers can find exactly what they're looking for with minimal effort. When customers land on your homepage, they should instantly understand where to go next. If they have to think too hard about how to find a product or navigate your menus, there's a good chance they'll abandon your site altogether. A well-structured website removes roadblocks and makes shopping effortless, guiding visitors naturally from browsing to checkout.

Organizing Product Categories The Right Way

One of the biggest mistakes I see store owners make is creating confusing or disorganized product categories. If shoppers can't quickly locate what they need, they're more likely to leave your store in frustration. Think of your website like a department store – products should be logically grouped in a way that makes sense to your customers. For example, if you sell clothing, your categories should be clear and distinct, like "Men's Apparel," "Women's Apparel," "Footwear," and "Accessories." Avoid using vague, overlapping, or redundant category names that could create confusion.

Another tip is to limit the number of main categories in your navigation menu. Too many choices can overwhelm shoppers and make decision-making harder. Instead, stick to broad, high-level categories and use subcategories to break things down further. If you have a large product catalog, consider adding a "New Arrivals" or "Best Sellers" section to help customers easily discover popular or trending items.

Improving Search With Smart Filtering Options

If your store has a large inventory, filters are

essential. Filters help customers refine their search results based on attributes like size, color, price, brand, or product type, making it easier to find what they want. Without filters, shoppers may have to scroll through hundreds of products, leading to frustration and higher bounce rates.

The key to effective filtering is keeping options relevant to your products. An electronics store, for example, should provide filters for "Screen Size," "Processor Type," and "Battery Life," while a home décor store might use filters for "Material," "Color," and "Style." Providing too many filter options can be overwhelming, so focus on the attributes that are most useful to your customers.

Learning From Industry Leaders

When in doubt, take a page from the playbook of major retailers like Amazon, Walmart, or Target. These companies have invested millions into refining their website navigation and user experience, and their success is built on making online shopping as seamless as possible. Their sites follow consistent design patterns – simple menus, prominent search bars, and clear category structures – that make it easy for users to shop without frustration.

One of the biggest lessons I've learned is that familiarity is better than novelty. Customers don't want to figure out a brand-new way to navigate an online store; they want something that they've seen before on other websites. That's why sticking to best practices – such as placing the shopping cart icon in the top right corner and keeping your main navigation consistent across all pages – helps create a better shopping experience. While it might be tempting to create a unique, artistic layout, remember that usability should always come first.

Best Practices for Mobile-Friendly Design

More than half of all online purchases are now made on mobile devices, making mobile-friendliness a critical factor in e-commerce success. If your store doesn't provide a smooth and intuitive shopping experience on mobile, you're likely losing a significant portion of potential sales. I've seen clients make small changes in mobile optimization that dramatically improved their conversion rates. Optimizing for smaller screens isn't just a good idea – it's a necessity.

Creating A Responsive Shopping Experience

A responsive design automatically adjusts its layout to fit the screen size of the device being used. This ensures that images, buttons, and text display correctly, regardless of whether a shopper is browsing on a phone, tablet, or desktop. A non-responsive site often leads to frustrating issues, like text that's too small to read, buttons that are impossible to tap, or images that don't scale properly. Customers who struggle with these problems won't stick around – they'll find another store that makes shopping easier.

Most modern e-commerce platforms, including Shopify and BigCommerce, offer mobile-responsive themes right out of the box. But even with a responsive design, it's important to test your site regularly on different devices to ensure everything functions smoothly. Load times, scrolling behavior, and the placement of key elements like the search bar and checkout button all play a role in creating a hassle-free mobile shopping experience. This is especially important if you've customized the design yourself – changes you make for the desktop design may not display properly on smaller screens without some CSS adjustments.

Designing For Touchscreens

Mobile users interact with websites by tapping and swiping rather than clicking, which means that every interactive element – like buttons, links, and form fields – needs to be optimized for touch. I often see buttons that are too small, making them difficult to tap accurately. Additionally, links should have enough spacing between them so users don't accidentally tap the wrong one.

Pay special attention to forms on mobile as well. Customers don't want to struggle with tiny input fields or deal with auto-correct errors when entering their email or shipping address. Form fields should be large enough to type into comfortably, and auto-correct should be disabled for email and password fields. Streamlining the checkout process by minimizing the number of required fields can also make a huge difference in reducing cart abandonment.

Simplifying the Mobile Checkout Process

A complicated or time-consuming checkout process is one of the biggest reasons shoppers abandon their carts, especially on mobile devices. Customers expect a quick and frictionless checkout experience, so it's essential to make the process as easy as possible. Offering guest checkout, auto-filling shipping details, and integrating digital wallets like Apple Pay and Google Pay can significantly improve mobile conversions.

Think about how often you've abandoned a cart simply because entering payment or shipping details felt like too much of a hassle on your phone. Eliminating unnecessary steps and allowing customers to complete their purchase with just a few taps removes obstacles and makes it easier for them to buy from you. The fewer barriers between browsing and purchasing, the higher your conversion rates will be.

How Site Speed Impacts Sales (and How to Improve It)

When it comes to running a successful online store, speed matters more than you might think. Studies have shown that even a one-second delay in page load time can reduce conversions by up to 7%.

If customers have to wait too long for a page to load, they're far more likely to abandon their cart and move on to a competitor. That's why improving site speed can lead to better engagement, lower bounce rates, and, most importantly, increased sales. A fast website not only keeps customers happy but also improves search engine rankings, helping drive more organic traffic to your store.

Optimizing Image Formats And Sizes

One of the most common causes of slow-loading websites is large, unoptimized images. While high-quality product photos are essential for e-commerce, oversized images can slow your site down significantly. The key is to strike a balance between quality and performance. In most cases, using JPG files instead of PNGs will help keep file sizes smaller without sacrificing image clarity. PNGs should only be used when transparency is required.

Another important tip is to upload images only in the maximum size needed. If your site displays product images at a maximum width of 800 pixels, there's no need to upload a 3000-pixel-wide version. In addition, compressing images before uploading them can make a big difference in load time. Tools like TinyPNG, ImageOptim, or Shopify's built-in image compression features can reduce file sizes without noticeably affecting quality. Taking these small steps can dramatically improve site speed without sacrificing the visual appeal of your store.

Reducing Unnecessary Scripts And Plugins

Many e-commerce platforms offer third-party apps and plugins to add extra functionality, but too many of these can slow your site down. Each additional script – whether it's for live chat, pop-ups, analytics, or marketing automation – adds extra load time. I recommend regularly auditing the plugins and scripts running on your store to determine what's truly necessary. If a feature isn't actively contributing to sales or improving the user experience, it might be worth removing.

If you're using Shopify, BigCommerce, or WooCommerce, take advantage of built-in performance features instead of relying on third-party apps whenever possible. Many speed issues arise when store owners unknowingly install multiple apps that serve similar purposes, leading to unnecessary bloat. Keeping things lean ensures your store runs as smoothly as possible.

Leveraging Browser Caching And Cdns

One of the simplest ways to speed up your website is by enabling browser caching. This allows returning visitors to load your site faster because elements like images, stylesheets, and scripts are stored locally on their device instead of being downloaded from scratch each time they visit. Most e-commerce platforms have caching settings available, and enabling them is a quick way to improve performance.

Another powerful tool is a Content Delivery Network (CDN). A CDN helps distribute your site's content across multiple servers around the world, ensuring that visitors always load your store from the server closest to their location. This reduces load times significantly, especially for international customers. Shopify and BigCommerce automatically include CDN functionality, while WooCommerce store owners can integrate CDNs like Cloudflare or Fastly for similar benefits.

HOMEPAGE DESIGN
& LAYOUT

What Makes a Great Homepage:
Clear Branding, CTAs, and Visuals

Your homepage is your store's digital front window. It's the first thing customers see when they land on your site, and it plays a major role in shaping their first impression. A well-designed homepage immediately communicates your brand's identity, makes navigation easy, and encourages visitors to take action – whether that's browsing products, signing up for an email list, or making a purchase. I've worked with many online store owners who overlooked the power of a strong homepage, but getting it right can mean the difference between a visitor bouncing in seconds or sticking around to shop.

Establishing Clear And Consistent Branding

Branding is what sets your store apart from competitors. A great homepage reinforces your brand's identity through a consistent visual style – everything from your logo and color scheme to your typography and imagery should feel cohesive. Think about how high-end fashion brands use sleek, minimalistic layouts with refined fonts, while a children's toy store might embrace bright colors and playful typography. Your design choices should reflect the personality of your business and connect with your ideal customers.

Beyond visuals, your homepage needs to communicate your value proposition right away. When someone lands on your site, they should instantly understand what you sell and why they should buy from you. A concise tagline or hero banner that highlights your unique selling points – such as "Handcrafted Jewelry, Ethically Made" or "Eco-Friendly Pet Supplies with Free Shipping" – helps differentiate your brand and builds trust with visitors. If customers have to guess what you offer, they're likely to leave before even exploring your products.

Using Calls To Action (Ctas) To Drive Engagement

Once visitors are on your homepage, you need to guide them toward taking action. Calls to action (CTAs) are the signposts that help direct customers where you want them to go. A strong CTA should be visually distinct – using contrasting colors that stand out without clashing with your overall design. The wording should be clear, action-oriented, and persuasive. For example:

"Shop Now"

"Get 10% Off – Subscribe Today"
"Discover New Arrivals"
"Limited-Time Offer – Buy Now"

While CTAs are essential, too many can create decision paralysis. I always recommend focusing on a primary CTA that stands out the most, with secondary CTAs placed strategically throughout the homepage. If your goal is to push sales, your "Shop Now" button should be front and center, while additional CTAs can promote things like newsletter sign-ups or featured product collections.

Structuring Your Homepage With A Strong Visual Hierarchy

A great homepage isn't just visually appealing – it follows a structured layout that naturally guides visitors through key sections. The most effective homepages use a clear visual hierarchy that directs attention where it's needed most. This often starts with a hero banner at the top of the page, featuring high-quality imagery or a short video that immediately captures attention. Below that, strategically placed sections can highlight featured categories, best-selling products, or limited-time promotions.

Whitespace is another critical element of homepage design. I've seen store owners cram their homepages with too much tightly packed information, making it visually overwhelming and difficult to navigate. By giving elements room to breathe, whitespace improves readability and helps customers absorb key messages without feeling bombarded. A clean layout makes your homepage feel professional, modern, and easy to use.

Think of your homepage as the foundation of your customer's journey – make it as inviting and intuitive as possible, and you'll see the results in your conversions and repeat visitors.

The Role of Featured Products and Promotions

Your homepage is also a strategic tool for driving sales. One of the best ways to maximize its potential is by featuring key products and promotions that catch visitors' attention right away. When a shopper lands on your site, they might not know exactly what they're looking for, so curating a selection of best sellers, trending items, and new arrivals helps guide them toward making a purchase. A well-placed promotion or featured product can be the nudge that turns a casual browser into a buyer.

Showcasing Best Sellers And New Arrivals

Think about the last time you walked into a retail store. The front displays often showcase the newest arrivals or the most popular products because retailers know that highlighting these items encourages more sales. The same principle applies to e-commerce. Your homepage should prominently display products that are either proven winners or new releases that you want to push.

For example, if you run a beauty store, a section labeled "Top 5 Skincare Picks" with high-quality images and short descriptions can help customers quickly identify in-demand products. An electronics store might have a "Trending Gadgets" section featuring limited-time offers on popular tech accessories. These featured sections create a sense of social proof – when shoppers see that an item is a best seller, they instinctively trust that it's worth buying.

But don't just pick random products to showcase. Your best sellers should be based on actual sales data, and new arrivals should align with seasonal trends or current customer interests. Rotating these sections periodically keeps your homepage fresh and gives returning customers a reason to explore.

Driving Urgency With Limited-Time Promotions

Promotions and discounts are some of the most effective ways to create urgency and encourage impulse purchases. A strategically placed promo banner on your homepage can have a significant impact on revenue. Flash sales, seasonal discounts, or limited-time offers can make customers feel like they need to act fast before they miss out. When appropriate, your homepage should include time-sensitive deals to create urgency, such as:

"Flash Sale – 24 Hours Only!"
"Buy One, Get One Free – This Weekend Only!"

"Holiday Sale – Up to 50% Off!"

Adding a countdown timer can amplify the effect, giving shoppers a visual cue that time is running out. But while promotions are powerful, they shouldn't take over your homepage. If every section is screaming for attention, visitors might feel overwhelmed of get the impression that your website is a discount outlet. Instead, promotions should complement the rest of your homepage content, appearing alongside featured collections and customer testimonials to create a balanced shopping experience.

Enhancing Engagement With Personalized Recommendations

Some of the biggest e-commerce brands have mastered the art of personalization, and there's a reason for that – it works. Personalized product recommendations make shoppers feel like the store understands their preferences, which increases both engagement and sales. By analyzing browsing history or past purchases, you can suggest relevant products that are more likely to lead to a purchase.

For example, if a customer has been browsing hiking gear, showing them a "Recommended for You" section featuring backpacks, water bottles, and trail shoes can make their shopping experience better. Personalized recommendations are especially effective for repeat customers, as they create a sense of familiarity and convenience.

If you're using an e-commerce platform like Shopify or BigCommerce, many apps and built-in tools can help automate these recommendations. Even a simple "Customers Also Bought" section can increase average order value by encouraging shoppers to add more items to their cart.

Keeping the Homepage Updated with Fresh Content

Your homepage is often the first impression customers have of your store, and if it looks outdated, it can send the wrong message. A stale homepage can make visitors question whether your store is still active or if they can trust you with their purchase. On the other hand, a homepage that's regularly updated shows that your business is thriving, introduces customers to new products and promotions, and even improves your search engine rankings. Search engines favor fresh content, so keeping your homepage dynamic can also help boost your SEO.

If we're thinking of your homepage as a storefront window, it should change with the seasons, showcase new arrivals, and highlight exciting promotions that make people want to step inside and browse. When visitors see that your store is constantly evolving, they'll be more likely to return, knowing they'll always find something new.

Here are some of the most effective ways to keep your homepage content fresh and relevant:

Seasonal Updates That Reflect
What's Happening Now

Shoppers love to see content that feels timely and relevant. Updating your homepage to reflect the current season, upcoming holidays, or major shopping events helps customers connect with your store and find products that match their needs. A "Spring Collection" banner in March or a "Black Friday Mega Sale" in November immediately signals to visitors that your store is active and in tune with what's happening in the retail world.

Seasonal updates don't have to be complicated. Even small tweaks – like changing homepage visuals, refreshing promotional messaging, or adjusting featured product selections – can make a big impact. The key is to align your homepage with what customers are looking for at that moment.

Featuring New Arrivals To Encourage Repeat Visits

Customers love discovering what's new, and your homepage is the perfect place to showcase fresh inventory. A "New Arrivals" section gives visitors a reason to keep coming back to see what's just been added. Even if they weren't planning to make a purchase, curiosity might lead them to explore.

For example, if you run a fashion store, featuring the latest styles for the season keeps your homepage relevant and exciting. If you sell tech gadgets, highlighting innovative new products can generate buzz and increase conversions. Keeping this section updated regularly ensures that both new and returning customers always have something interesting to check out.

Building Trust With Customer Reviews & Testimonials

A homepage that feels static and impersonal can make customers hesitant to buy, but featuring real customer experiences brings it to life. Adding customer reviews, testimonials, or user-generated content (like photos of happy customers using your products) helps build trust and makes your store feel more dynamic.

Seeing a positive review front and center can be the reassurance a shopper needs to make a purchase. A simple section like "What Our Customers Are Saying" with rotating testimonials or star ratings next to featured products can instantly add credibility to your brand.

Integrating A Blog To Provide Value And Boost Seo

If your store has a blog, incorporating it into your homepage can provide additional value for visitors while also helping with SEO. Featuring recent articles or guides that align with your products can keep your homepage content fresh and encourage engagement.

For instance, if you sell fitness gear, highlighting a blog post like "5 Essential Items for Your Home Gym" can provide helpful information while subtly promoting your products. If you run a beauty store, a featured post on "Skincare Trends to Watch This Season" can position your store as an authority in your niche while keeping visitors engaged.

HOW TO CREATE EFFECTIVE LANDING PAGES THAT CONVERT

A landing page isn't just another page on your website – it's a strategic tool designed to drive a specific action. Unlike your homepage, which serves multiple purposes, a landing page is laser-focused on one objective. Whether you're capturing leads, promoting a product launch, or running a limited-time offer, the key to a high-converting landing page is eliminating distractions and guiding visitors toward a single call to action.

Think about the difference between a landing page and a standard webpage. If someone lands on your homepage, they have multiple pathways to explore – your navigation menu, product categories, blog content, and more. A landing page, however, removes all the noise. It's built to funnel visitors toward one clear goal. For example, if you're launching a limited-edition sneaker, your landing page should focus entirely on getting visitors to pre-order now. If you run a subscription business, your landing page should emphasize a free trial sign-up, with compelling reasons why visitors should take action immediately.

Essential Elements of a High-Converting Landing Page

A great landing page taps into psychology, persuasion, and user experience. Every element should work together to build trust, engage visitors, and drive conversions.

Crafting A Compelling Headline

The headline is the first thing visitors see, so it needs to grab their attention instantly. A strong headline clearly communicates value and sparks interest. Instead of something generic like "Welcome to Our Store", aim for a benefit-driven statement like:

"The Softest Sheets You'll Ever Sleep On – 20% Off Today Only!"

"Transform Your Skin in 7 Days – Try Our Best-Selling Serum Risk-Free!"

"Step Into Comfort – The Most Lightweight Sneakers You'll Ever Own"

A great headline immediately tells visitors what's in it for them. If they have to guess why they should care, you've already lost them.

Engaging Visuals That Build Trust

People process images faster than text, which

is why high-quality visuals are essential on landing pages. Whether it's product images, lifestyle photography, or a short video demonstrating your product in action, visuals should reinforce the message you're communicating.

For example, if you're selling premium cookware, an image of a beautifully plated meal prepared with your pots and pans will be far more effective than just a picture of the cookware itself. Showcasing real-life use cases makes your product more relatable and desirable.

Persuasive Copy That Focuses On Benefits

One mistake I see all the time is brands focusing too much on product features rather than benefits. Features are important, but they don't necessarily tell customers why they should care. Instead of saying "Made with organic cotton", a more persuasive description would be "Experience luxurious, breathable comfort with eco-friendly, organic cotton bedding". The second version paints a picture of what the product actually feels like for the customer. Many store owners consider this type of content "fluff", but it can actually have a substantial impact on conversion.

Use concise, benefit-driven copy that answers the question, "How will this improve my life?" Bullet points can be helpful here, but they should highlight advantages, not just technical details.

Building Trust With Social Proof

Trust is a huge factor in whether someone decides to convert on a landing page. People want reassurance that they're making a good decision, and one of the best ways to provide that is through social proof. Incorporating customer reviews, testimonials, media mentions, or security badges (such as "100% Satisfaction Guaranteed") helps reduce skepticism.

If you have glowing reviews, highlight them prominently. A simple "What Our Customers Are Saying" section with star ratings and real testimonials can significantly boost conversions. If your product has been featured in well-known publications, an "As Seen In" section adds credibility.

Creating An Irresistible Call To Action (Cta)

The call to action (CTA) is the most critical part of your landing page. It needs to be clear, bold, and action-oriented. Rather than a bland "Submit" button, use engaging language that drives urgency and excitement, such as:

"Get Yours Today"
"Claim Your Discount Now"
"Try It Risk-Free"

The placement of your CTA is just as important as the wording. It should be above the fold (meaning visible without scrolling) and repeated throughout the page in case visitors need more convincing before taking action.

PRODUCT PAGE OPTIMIZATION

Your product page is where the final buying decision happens. It's the moment when a customer either clicks "Add to Cart" or walks away. A well-optimized product page doesn't just display information; it actively guides shoppers toward making a purchase. I've seen too many e-commerce stores treat product pages as simple placeholders, but in reality, they should be built strategically to reduce friction, build trust, and create urgency. Every detail matters, from the way you name your products to how you present pricing and shipping details.

How to Create an Effective Product Page

Craft Clear And Descriptive Product Titles

Your product title is one of the first things a shopper sees, and it also plays a huge role in SEO. A vague title like "Leather Jacket" won't do much to help customers or search engines understand what you're selling. Instead, a more detailed and optimized title – such as "Men's Classic Black Leather

Biker Jacket – Genuine Leather" – provides clarity while naturally incorporating relevant keywords. If you only sell one type of product, such as handcrafted soap or candles, remember to include the product type in the name. Don't just say "Lavender", say "Lavender Hand Soap".

Think about how people search for products. They're often looking for something specific, like a "waterproof hiking backpack" or a "stainless steel French press." A well-crafted title should match how customers describe the product in their minds while still being concise and easy to read.

Use Strong And Actionable Calls To Action (Ctas)

If there's one thing I always emphasize to store owners, it's that your Add to Cart or Buy Now button needs to stand out. Your CTA should be bold, high-contrast, and positioned prominently on the page – because if a customer has to search for it, you're losing sales.

Beyond visibility, the wording of your CTA can matter. Instead of a generic "Add to Cart", you can try something more action-driven like "Get Yours Today", "Limited Stock – Order Now", or "Claim Your Deal". Adding urgency can make a significant difference in conversion rates, especially when paired with stock availability indicators or time-sensitive offers.

Display Pricing And Discounts Effectively

Pricing should never be an afterthought. Customers should be able to find the price instantly, and any discounts or special offers should be highly visible. If you're running a sale, showing the original price alongside the discounted price reinforces the value of the deal. For example:

Original Price: $99.99
Sale Price: $79.99 (20% Off)

Another powerful strategy is to highlight savings in a way that makes the discount feel more significant. Instead of simply listing the new price, emphasizing phrases like "Save $20 Today!" or "Limited-Time Offer – 20% Off!" can encourage quicker purchasing decisions.

Address Shipping And Return Concerns Upfront

Shipping costs and return policies are among the biggest reasons customers hesitate at checkout. If they can't easily find shipping details or worry about returns, they might abandon their cart. That's why I always recommend placing key shipping information near the product price or CTA. For example:

"Free Shipping on Orders Over $50"
"Ships in 2-3 Business Days"
"30-Day Hassle-Free Returns"

Transparency builds confidence. If customers know exactly what to expect, they're far less likely to second-guess their decision before completing the purchase.

Create Urgency With Stock Availability And Scarcity Indicators

Scarcity is a powerful psychological trigger. If customers believe an item might sell out soon, they're more likely to act immediately rather than delay their purchase. Adding stock availability indicators – such as "Only 3 Left in Stock!" – can increase the sense of urgency.

Limited-time offers and countdown timers can also be effective. A simple message like "Flash Sale Ends in 3 Hours!" or a ticking countdown clock next to the discount price can push hesitant shoppers to take action before they miss out.

Writing Compelling Product Descriptions

A great product description does more than just list details – it tells a story, evokes emotion, and convinces customers that they need this product in their lives. I've seen too many e-commerce stores treat descriptions as an afterthought, providing dry, technical specs without any personality. The truth is, a well-crafted description can be the deciding factor between a customer hitting "Buy Now" or leaving your site.

Focus On Benefits, Not Just Features

One of the most common mistakes I see is

product descriptions that read like a spec sheet. While features are important, customers don't just want to know what a product is – they want to know why it matters. How will it improve their life? How will it solve a problem? For example, compare these two descriptions for a leather jacket:

Feature-focused: "This jacket is made of 100% genuine leather."

Benefit-focused: "Crafted from 100% genuine leather, this jacket offers unmatched durability and a sleek, modern style perfect for any occasion. Whether you're heading out for a night on the town or layering up for a casual day out, this jacket elevates your look effortlessly."

The second description doesn't just state a fact – it paints a picture of how the product fits into the customer's lifestyle. That's the kind of messaging that converts.

Make Descriptions Easy To Scan

People don't read product pages like novels – they skim. That's why formatting is just as important as the words you use. Breaking up descriptions into short paragraphs and highlighting key points makes it easier for shoppers to digest the information quickly.

If you're listing multiple benefits, using bullet points can make scanning even easier. For example, instead of a large block of text, format it like this:

- Premium genuine leather for long-lasting wear
- Slim-fit design for a modern, stylish look
- Adjustable waist belt for a customized fit
- Soft inner lining for added comfort

This approach ensures that even customers who are just skimming the page can quickly grasp why the product is worth buying.

Incorporate Storytelling To Make Products More Relatable

The best product descriptions make customers feel something. Adding a little storytelling makes the product more relatable and engaging. Instead of just listing features, describe how the product was created, the inspiration behind it, or how it fits into the customer's lifestyle.

For example, if you're selling handmade candles, instead of saying:

"This candle is made with all-natural soy wax."

Try this:

"Inspired by cozy autumn evenings, our hand-poured cinnamon vanilla candle fills your home with warm, inviting aromas. Made with all-natural soy wax and infused with essential oils, it's the perfect way to unwind after a long day."

By creating an experience in the customer's mind, you make the product feel more valuable and desirable.

Optimize For Seo

A well-written product description also helps search engines find your product. The key is to incorporate relevant keywords naturally, without forcing them in awkwardly. Think about the phrases your customers are actually searching for, like "best leather jackets for men" or "eco-friendly soy candles." Including these terms in a way that feels conversational and authentic makes your product more discoverable without compromising readability.

For example, instead of writing:

"Our best leather jackets for men are high-quality. If you want the best leather jackets for men, shop here!"

Try something more natural:

"Looking for a high-quality leather jacket that's both stylish and durable? Our expertly crafted men's leather jackets are designed for comfort and long-lasting wear."

This approach helps your product rank better in search results while still providing a smooth, engaging experience for customers.

The Power of High-Quality

Images and Videos

When shopping online, customers can't pick up, try on, or physically inspect a product like they would in a store. That's why high-quality visuals are critical to bridging the gap between digital browsing and real-life confidence in a purchase. I've worked with many store owners who underestimated the impact of strong visuals, only to see their conversions improve dramatically once they upgraded their product images and videos.

A product page without compelling images is like a sales pitch without enthusiasm. Customers need to see the details, textures, and real-life applications of a product before they feel comfortable making a purchase. High-quality visuals don't just enhance aesthetics – they build trust, reduce uncertainty, and improve overall user experience.

Use High-Resolution Images To Build Confidence

Blurry or pixelated images make a product look cheap, no matter how high-quality it actually is. Customers associate image quality with product quality, so investing in high-resolution images is one of the simplest and most effective ways to increase conversions. Every product should have multiple images from different angles, showcasing its full design and features.

For example, a clothing retailer should include front, back, and side views of an item, along with close-ups of details like stitching, buttons, and fabric textures. A home decor store can benefit from showing how a piece looks in different lighting or styled within a space. When customers can zoom in to inspect details or interact with 360-degree views, it replicates the in-store experience and provides the confidence needed to complete a purchase.

Another powerful technique is using lifestyle photography to show products in action. A camping gear store, for instance, could feature images of tents set up in scenic locations or backpacks being worn on a trail. This approach helps customers visualize themselves using the product, making the purchase feel more personal and aspirational.

Leverage Videos To Showcase Product Functionality

While high-quality images are essential, video content takes things a step further. Videos allow you to demonstrate product functionality, answer potential customer questions, and create a more immersive shopping experience.

A short product demo video can highlight key features in ways that photos simply can't. For example:

- A fashion brand can show how a dress flows when walking or how a jacket fits on different body types.

- An electronics store can demonstrate how a gadget works, showcasing features like touchscreen responsiveness or ease of setup.

- A furniture retailer can use video to show how easily a sofa converts into a bed or how sturdy a table is under weight.

Another possible strategy is unboxing videos. Many major brands use unboxing videos to showcase packaging, product components, and first impressions – giving customers a clearer idea of what to expect. If you sell a premium product, highlighting the unboxing experience can reinforce its value.

Leveraging Customer Reviews For Social Proof

One of the biggest hurdles in e-commerce is convincing potential buyers to trust your products without being able to see or try them in person. That's where customer reviews come in. Reviews act as digital word-of-mouth, providing shoppers with real-life insights from people who have already purchased the product. I've seen firsthand how adding even a handful of reviews to a product page can significantly boost conversions, and research backs this up. Products with reviews convert 270% more than those without.

Why Reviews Matter

Think about the last time you bought something online. Did you check the reviews first? If you're like most shoppers, the answer is yes. Reviews provide reassurance, address common concerns, and offer perspectives that product descriptions simply can't replicate. A great review can highlight unexpected benefits, confirm quality, or even answer a question another potential buyer might have.

Even critical reviews play a role. Customers don't expect perfection, but they do want honesty. A mix of glowing feedback and constructive criticism builds credibility and helps customers make informed decisions. Plus, having a transparent review system conveys that your store values customer opinions, reinforcing trust in your brand.

Encouraging Customers To Leave Reviews

While reviews are incredibly valuable, most customers won't leave one unless prompted. That's why automating review requests is essential. Setting up an email that goes out 7-10 days after the product is delivered increases the likelihood that a customer will take the time to share their experience.

A simple, well-crafted email can make all the difference. Keep the request short and friendly, thanking them for their purchase and inviting them to leave a quick review. If you want to increase participation, consider offering a small incentive, such as a discount on their next purchase or bonus points if you have a rewards program.

Another way to boost engagement is to make the review process as simple as possible. Using a review app that allows customers to submit one-click star ratings directly from the email increases response rates. Giving them the option to provide written feedback but not requiring it makes it less of a hassle for them to participate.

Displaying Reviews For Maximum Impact

Once you start collecting reviews, it's crucial to display them effectively. Reviews should be highly visible on the product page. A star rating should appear near the top, next to the product title, so customers immediately see social proof. Below that, a link to "Read All Reviews" makes it easy for shoppers to browse feedback.

When possible, feature customer reviews that include images or videos. Seeing real people using the product adds an extra layer of trust and authenticity. Many review apps also offer verified purchase badges, which help establish credibility by showing that the reviewer actually bought the product from your store.

It's also important to allow a mix of positive and constructive reviews. While you can (and should) reject spam or irrelevant reviews, customers are more likely to trust your store if they see honest feedback – even if it's not all five-star ratings. If a review points out a small issue but also praises the product overall, that can actually reassure buyers that they're getting an unbiased perspective.

Incorporating User-Generated Content For Social Proof

One of the most powerful ways to build trust is by encouraging customers to submit photos and videos of themselves using your products. This takes social proof to the next level because it shows real people integrating the product into their daily lives.

Successful brands often create a "See It In Action" section on product pages, featuring user-submitted images and videos. This not only enhances credibility but also provides a community-driven feel, where new customers see others enjoying the product and feel more confident in their purchase decision.

CHECKOUT PROCESS & CART ABANDONMENT REDUCTION

The checkout process is where all your hard work – your marketing, your product pages, your customer engagement – either pays off or falls apart. It's the final step in the buying journey, and if there's too much friction, customers will abandon their carts and walk away. In fact, nearly 70% of online shopping carts are abandoned, often because of unnecessary complications during checkout. That's a staggering number, and it highlights just how crucial it is to create a smooth, intuitive experience that makes completing a purchase as easy as possible.

I've seen many store owners unintentionally lose sales by adding too many elements to their checkouts. If customers have to jump through hoops, fill out too many fields, or struggle with an inefficient layout, they'll leave – no matter how much they love the product. That's why streamlining checkout is one of the most effective ways to boost conversions and keep customers coming back.

Reduce Steps to Make Checkout Effortless

One of the easiest ways to improve checkout is by minimizing the number of steps required to complete a purchase. A long, multi-step checkout process can feel overwhelming – especially on mobile devices. The best approach is to consolidate fields and, if possible, present everything on a single page so customers don't have to keep clicking through different sections.

If multiple steps are necessary, adding a progress indicator reassures customers by showing them exactly where they are in the process. This small change can help reduce frustration and keep buyers engaged. Additionally, auto-fill and predictive typing can significantly cut down on manual input, making checkout faster and more convenient. Most modern browsers and mobile devices support these features, so enabling them for shipping and payment fields is a simple but impactful improvement.

Ask for Only the Essentials

A big reason customers abandon checkout is because they're asked for too much information. While it might be tempting to gather additional data – like phone numbers, or how they heard of your store – every extra field creates another barrier to completing the purchase. The key is to only ask for what's absolutely necessary: shipping and billing details, payment information, and an email for order confirmation.

If you want to collect additional information, do it after the purchase – not during checkout. Optional fields, such as newsletter sign-ups or feedback forms, should never disrupt the buying process. Let customers opt in once their order is placed.

Make Checkout Mobile-Friendly

With mobile commerce on the rise, checkout must be designed with mobile users in mind. A form that works fine on a desktop might be frustrating on a smartphone. To ensure an easy experience, make sure your checkout includes:

- Larger buttons and tap-friendly elements for easy navigation.
- Auto-detection for credit card numbers and addresses to speed up form completion.
- Mobile-optimized payment options like Apple Pay, Google Pay, and PayPal, which eliminate the need for customers to manually enter billing details.

A mobile-friendly checkout removes friction so customers can buy without frustration. The easier it is to check out on a phone, the more sales you'll capture.

Offer Guest Checkout to

Remove Login Barriers

Forcing customers to create an account before purchasing is one of the quickest ways to lose a sale. While account creation has its benefits – like enabling order tracking and future marketing – it shouldn't be a requirement. Guest checkout should always be an option so that first-time customers don't feel forced into an extra step they weren't expecting.

A great compromise is to offer account creation after checkout. For example, once a customer completes their purchase, you can present an option like, "Create an account to save your order history and track shipments". This gives them the choice without interrupting their buying experience.

Payment Options and Security Considerations

One of the easiest ways to lose a sale is by not offering the right payment options. Customers want convenience, and if they don't see their preferred payment method at checkout, they might abandon their cart entirely. I've worked with many store owners who saw an immediate boost in conversions just by expanding their payment options. The key is to provide a seamless and secure payment experience that caters to different preferences while ensuring customers feel confident in completing their purchase.

Offering A Variety Of Payment Methods

Different customers prefer different ways to pay, and limiting your payment options means leaving money on the table. While credit and debit cards remain the most widely used methods, supporting multiple card providers – such as Visa, MasterCard, American Express, and Discover – ensures broad accessibility.

However, today's shoppers expect more than just traditional card payments. Digital wallets like Apple Pay, Google Pay, and PayPal have become increasingly popular, particularly among mobile users who want to check out quickly without manually entering their card details. These options make checkout faster and more convenient.

Another popular option for e-commerce businesses is Buy Now, Pay Later (BNPL) services like Klarna, Afterpay, and Affirm. These allow customers to split their purchase into manageable installments, making higher-priced items more accessible. If your store sells products with a higher price point – electronics, fashion, or furniture, for example – offering BNPL can significantly boost conversions. Some stores even cater to niche audiences by accepting cryptocurrency or alternative payment methods, further broadening their customer base.

Reinforcing Trust And Security In Payments

Customers won't enter their payment details unless they trust your site. Reassuring shoppers that their transaction is secure is just as important as offering multiple payment options. Small trust signals go a long way in making them feel comfortable entering their credit card details.

Displaying SSL encryption certification, recognizable payment provider logos, and "Secure Checkout" badges reassures buyers that their data is protected. These elements should be placed near the checkout form, where customers can see them before completing their purchase. Additionally, ensuring that your store's domain uses HTTPS encryption prevents browser warnings that could scare away potential buyers.

Preventing Fraud While Maintaining A Smooth Experience

While making checkout simple is essential, security should never be compromised. Fraud prevention measures help protect your business from chargebacks and unauthorized transactions while keeping your customers' data safe. A few best practices include:

- Address Verification System (AVS) checks: This ensures that the billing address entered matches what the payment provider has on file, reducing the risk of fraudulent transactions.

- Requiring Card Verification Value (CVV): Asking for the CVV (the three or four-digit code on a credit card) adds an extra layer of security and makes it harder for fraudsters to use stolen card numbers.

- Implementing 3D Secure authentication: Services like Visa Secure and Mastercard Identity Check require customers to verify their identity with an additional step, such as a one-time passcode sent to their phone. While an extra step in the process might sound inconvenient, it can significantly reduce chargeback risks and increase transaction security.

DESIGNING FOR SEO AND ACCESSIBILITY

How Web Design Affects SEO Rankings

Many store owners focus on SEO as a separate task from web design, but in reality, they are deeply connected. A well-structured, SEO-friendly website is about making sure that search engines can easily understand and index your content. I've seen too many businesses struggle with poor search rankings simply because their site design wasn't optimized for SEO. If your site structure is confusing, your pages load slowly, or your content isn't formatted properly, search engines won't rank your store as high as it deserves.

One of the most important factors in SEO-friendly web design is site structure. A clear and logical layout helps customers navigate easily while also making it easier for search engines to crawl and index your pages. E-commerce stores should have a well-organized category and subcategory system, ensuring that every product page is reachable with minimal clicks. Internal linking between related products and blog content strengthens connections between pages, boosting rankings. Additionally, breadcrumb navigation improves usability by showing visitors exactly where they are on your site while also helping search engines understand the site's hierarchy.

Why Page Speed Matters For Seo

If there's one technical factor that directly impacts both user experience and SEO, it's page speed. A slow-loading website doesn't just frustrate visitors – it leads to higher bounce rates, which signals to Google that your site isn't providing a good experience. Studies show that customers expect pages to load in three seconds or less, and every extra second of delay increases the likelihood they'll leave without purchasing.

So how do you speed up your site? Compressing images, minifying CSS and JavaScript, and enabling browser caching are some of the most effective ways to improve load times. Many e-commerce platforms also have built-in tools to optimize speed, so take advantage of them. Google's Core Web Vitals, which measure key aspects of site performance, now play a crucial role in search rankings. Ensuring that your site passes these performance metrics can help you rank higher in search results while keeping customers engaged.

The Role Of Mobile Responsiveness In Search Rankings

With mobile commerce dominating online shopping, Google now prioritizes mobile-friendly websites in its rankings. If your site isn't responsive – meaning it doesn't automatically adjust to different screen sizes – you'll struggle to rank well in search results. More importantly, you'll lose customers. Nobody wants to pinch and zoom just to navigate a website.

A responsive design ensures that everything – images, buttons, menus, and checkout forms – functions properly on smartphones and tablets. In fact, Google's mobile-first indexing means that it evaluates your mobile site first, rather than your desktop version, when determining rankings. If your mobile experience is lacking, your SEO will suffer. Regularly test your site on different devices to make sure it looks great and loads quickly, no matter how customers are shopping.

Optimizing On-Page Seo Elements Through Design

SEO-friendly design isn't just about technical factors – it also includes how you structure and present your content. Using proper HTML tags for headings (H1, H2, H3) helps both users and search engines understand the structure of your pages. For example, your product title should always be wrapped in an H1 tag, while subheadings within product descriptions or blog posts should use H2 and H3 tags for clarity.

Other on-page elements, such as meta descriptions, play a huge role in getting customers to click on your store in search results. A compelling meta description that includes relevant keywords can significantly improve click-through rates (CTR). Additionally, implementing structured data markup helps search engines display rich snippets, such as product ratings, pricing, and stock availability, directly in search results – making your listings more attractive and informative for potential buyers.

Image Optimization and Alt Text

Images are one of the most powerful tools in e-commerce. They showcase your products, build customer confidence, and ultimately help drive sales. However, if they're not optimized properly, they can also slow down your site, hurt your search rankings, and frustrate potential buyers. I've worked with plenty of store owners who were unknowingly losing customers because their product images were too large, loaded too slowly, or weren't optimized for accessibility. We've covered some of these tips in previous chapters, but they're worth revisiting in more detail.

Balancing Image Quality And Performance

High-resolution images are essential for making your products look great, but they also need to be compressed to keep your website fast. Large, unoptimized images are one of the biggest reasons for slow-loading pages, and we know that customers won't wait long – if a page takes more than three seconds to load, many shoppers will leave.

To prevent slowdowns, I recommend uploading images no larger than 1500x1500 pixels and using image compression tools like TinyPNG or ImageOptim. These tools significantly reduce file sizes while maintaining visual quality, ensuring that your site loads quickly without sacrificing the sharpness of your product images.

Choosing The Right Image Format

The file format you use plays a major role in both image quality and page speed. JPEG is generally the best option for e-commerce product images because it maintains good quality at a relatively small file size. PNG files, while higher in quality, should only be used when transparency is necessary – such as logos or graphics with clear backgrounds. A more modern alternative is WebP, a format that provides even better compression without losing quality, and is increasingly supported by modern browsers. If your e-commerce platform allows it, switching to WebP can help improve page speed without compromising on visuals.

Optimizing Image Filenames For Seo

Many store owners overlook this simple but powerful SEO trick: naming image files correctly. Instead of uploading a product photo with a default filename like "IMG_1234.jpg," rename it to something descriptive and keyword-rich, like "red-leather-handbag.jpg." Search engines can't "see" images the way humans do, so filenames provide valuable context that helps improve rankings in image search results.

Using Alt Text For Accessibility And Seo

Alt text (alternative text) is a critical component of image optimization, and it serves two important purposes: it makes your site more accessible to visually impaired users and it improves your search engine rankings. Screen readers rely on alt text to describe images to users who can't see them, and search engines use alt text to understand the content of your images.

A well-written alt text description should be concise yet descriptive. Instead of writing something vague like "handbag", a better alt text example would be: "Red leather handbag with gold chain strap, perfect for evening wear." This description not only helps users relying on screen readers but also includes keywords that can improve your SEO. However, don't "keyword stuff" your alt tags with keywords that don't accurately describe the photo just for SEO purposes – that will have a negative impact on your website's accessibility.

Enhancing Performance With Lazy Loading And Smart Image Usage

Beyond individual product images, optimizing

thumbnails and product galleries can also enhance site speed. While multiple images provide customers with a better look at your products, excessive image carousels can slow down load times. Lazy loading – a technique where images only load when they come into view – can significantly boost performance without reducing image quality.

Making Your Store Accessible to All Customers

Ensuring that your e-commerce store is accessible to all customers isn't just about meeting compliance standards – it's about creating an inclusive shopping experience that benefits everyone. A well-designed, accessible website not only expands your customer base but also improves usability, boosts engagement, and even enhances your SEO rankings. I've worked with many store owners who initially overlooked accessibility, only to realize later that making their site more inclusive led to a noticeable increase in conversions and customer satisfaction.

Web accessibility means making your store usable for people with a range of disabilities, including vision impairments, hearing impairments, mobility limitations, and cognitive challenges. By implementing accessibility best practices, you ensure that every potential customer – regardless of ability – can navigate, browse, and complete purchases with ease.

Improving Readability For Better Accessibility

One of the most effective ways to enhance accessibility is by making sure your text is easy to read. Font sizes should be large enough for comfortable reading, and contrast ratios should be high enough to make text stand out against the background. The Web Content Accessibility Guidelines (WCAG) recommend a contrast ratio of at least 4.5:1 for normal text, which means avoiding light gray text on a white background or neon-colored text on dark backgrounds. Clear, high-contrast text improves readability for everyone – not just those with visual impairments.

Additionally, using simple and concise language benefits all users, particularly those with cognitive disabilities. Overly complex descriptions or jargon can make it harder for some shoppers to understand product details. By keeping content straightforward and well-organized, you create a smoother browsing experience for all customers.

Enhancing Navigation For Keyboard Users

Not all users navigate with a mouse – many rely on keyboard navigation, especially those with mobility impairments. To ensure accessibility, your store should allow users to navigate through interactive elements (such as menus, links, and buttons) using only a keyboard. The Tab key should move logically from one element to the next, and each focused item should have a clearly visible focus indicator to show where the user is on the page.

Forms should also be fully accessible. Every input field should have a visible and properly associated label, as placeholder text alone is often not recognized by screen readers. This helps users understand what information they need to enter, improving both accessibility and overall usability.

Providing Text Alternatives For Non-Text Content

Many shoppers rely on screen readers or other assistive technologies to navigate websites. That's why text alternatives for non-text content are essential. Every image should have descriptive alt text, explaining what the image shows. Instead of labeling an image as "shirt," a more helpful description would be "blue cotton t-shirt with a V-neck and short sleeves." This approach improves both accessibility and SEO since search engines also use alt text to understand images.

Videos should include captions for users with hearing impairments, ensuring they can access the information even without audio. If you use instructional videos, providing a transcript is also helpful for users who prefer reading over watching.

Creating Clear And Helpful Error Messages

A frustrating checkout experience can drive customers away – especially if error messages are vague or unhelpful. If a user makes a mistake while filling out a form, they should receive a clear and actionable error message. Instead of saying "Invalid input," a more useful message would be "Please enter a valid email address in the format example@domain.com." Giving customers clear guidance prevents frustration and helps them complete their purchase smoothly.

How Accessibility And Seo Work Together

Many accessibility best practices also improve search engine optimization (SEO), making your store more visible in search results. Properly structured headings (H1, H2, H3, etc.) improve navigation for both users and search engines. A well-organized layout, descriptive alt text, and clear labels make your site easier for search engines to crawl, leading to better rankings and increased organic traffic.

Additionally, websites with strong user experience signals – such as low bounce rates, fast load times, and mobile-friendly design – tend to rank higher in search results. Since accessibility improvements often align with usability enhancements, prioritizing accessibility can have a direct impact on your store's SEO performance.

LEVERAGING APPS & PLUGINS WITHOUT OVERLOADING YOUR SITE

Essential Plugins for SaaS E-Commerce Platforms

One of the biggest advantages of using a SaaS (Software as a Service) e-commerce platform, like Shopify, BigCommerce, or WooCommerce, is the ability to extend functionality through apps and plugins. While these platforms come with a strong set of built-in features, it's often the right combination of plugins that transforms a store from basic to high-performing. I've seen store owners drastically improve their sales, efficiency, and customer experience simply by choosing the right tools.

That said, it's important to be selective. Too many plugins can slow down your site and create unnecessary complexity, so you'll want to focus on those that provide the most value without negatively impacting performance.

Optimizing Seo And Marketing

Driving organic traffic is essential for e-commerce success, and SEO plugins help ensure your store is discoverable by search engines. If you're using WooCommerce, a plugin like Yoast SEO can help optimize your product pages, meta descriptions, and sitemaps. For Shopify, an app like Plug In SEO automates SEO checks and suggests improvements. These tools help store owners fine-tune their content, improving rankings and increasing visibility.

Email marketing is another essential component of an effective e-commerce strategy. Integrating tools like Klaviyo or Omnisend allows you to automate abandoned cart emails, segment customers for targeted promotions, and increase repeat purchases. With these apps, you can build smarter email campaigns that drive revenue while keeping your brand top of mind for customers.

Enhancing Checkout And Payment Options

One of the biggest reasons for cart abandonment is a complicated or limited checkout process. While SaaS platforms come with standard payment gateways, integrating additional options can improve conversions.

Stripe and PayPal integrations ensure customers can check out quickly using their preferred method, while Buy Now, Pay Later (BNPL) services like

Klarna, Afterpay, or Affirm give customers more flexibility by allowing them to split their purchase into installments. Many shoppers expect these options, and offering them can significantly boost order values.

Improving Customer Support And Engagement

Providing excellent customer support is crucial in building trust and loyalty. Adding a live chat tool like Tidio or Gorgias allows you to provide real-time assistance, answering questions before they lead to abandoned carts. AI-powered chatbots can even handle basic inquiries automatically, ensuring customers receive quick responses at all times.

Another powerful engagement tool is customer loyalty and rewards programs. Apps like Smile.io allow you to set up point-based rewards, encouraging repeat purchases and increasing customer retention. Additionally, review collection tools like Yotpo or Judge.me help showcase authentic customer feedback, which boosts credibility and conversions.

Automating Inventory And Order Management

As an online store grows, inventory management becomes increasingly complex. The right plugins can sync inventory across multiple sales channels, ensuring you don't oversell or run out of stock unexpectedly. Apps like Orderhive or Stock Sync automate inventory tracking, reducing errors and making fulfillment more efficient.

Shipping and logistics plugins like ShipStation or Easyship integrate with multiple carriers, offering real-time shipping rates and automated tracking updates. These tools help streamline fulfillment, allowing you to provide faster and more transparent shipping options for customers.

Choosing The Right Plugins For Your Store

With thousands of apps available, it's easy to get carried away. However, installing too many plugins can slow down your website, create compatibility issues, and complicate management. I always recommend taking a "less is more" approach – choose plugins that align directly with your business goals and streamline essential operations. A great way to decide which plugins to use is to ask yourself:

- Does this plugin improve customer experience or increase sales?

- Will this tool save time or automate an essential task?

- Is it well-reviewed and compatible with my e-commerce platform?

By prioritizing functionality over quantity, you can build a high-performing, efficient, and customer-friendly online store that's equipped for long-term success.

Avoiding Slowdowns from Excessive App Usage

While plugins and apps can dramatically enhance your store's functionality, installing too many can slow down your site and create performance issues. Each app runs its own scripts and background processes, which can negatively impact page load speed, user experience, and even SEO rankings.

The first step in preventing slowdowns is to conduct a plugin audit. Many store owners install apps for testing or temporary needs and forget to remove them after they're no longer useful. Regularly reviewing and deactivating unused plugins helps keep your site lean and efficient. SaaS platforms like Shopify and BigCommerce have built-in app management dashboards, making it easy to disable or delete redundant apps.

Another common issue is apps that load scripts across the entire site, even when they're only needed on specific pages. For example, a live chat widget should only load on product and checkout pages rather than every page on your site. Tools like Google PageSpeed Insights or GTmetrix can help identify scripts that may be causing performance issues.

It's also important to avoid duplicating functionality. Some store owners unknowingly install multiple apps that perform the same tasks, such as using two different abandoned cart recovery tools. Instead, choose a single, well-rounded solution that meets your needs without unnecessary redundancy.

Reducing reliance on external scripts and third-party APIs can further improve site speed. Many plugins fetch data from external servers, which increases the number of HTTP requests. If possible, prioritize apps that handle processes internally rather than relying on constant external calls.

For WooCommerce users, optimizing hosting and implementing server-side caching strategies can also help mitigate the impact of plugins. Using a Content Delivery Network (CDN), optimizing database queries, and enabling browser caching can improve site speed while still allowing for robust functionality.

Finally, before installing any new plugin, test its impact on website performance. Many platforms allow for staging environments where you can try out an app before making it live. Running speed tests before and after installation ensures you're not unintentionally introducing lag to your store.

CONCLUSION: BRINGING IT ALL TOGETHER

Recap of Best Practices

Throughout this book, we've explored the key elements of effective web design for SaaS e-commerce platforms, covering everything from homepage optimization and checkout best practices to leveraging third-party apps and ensuring accessibility. If there's one overarching takeaway, it's that a well-designed website isn't just about aesthetics – it's about functionality, user experience, and driving conversions.

A high-performing e-commerce site removes friction at every step, ensuring that customers can browse products, find information, and complete purchases without unnecessary obstacles. When done correctly, web design guides the customer journey, builds trust, and ultimately increases sales.

Creating A Seamless Shopping Experience

A successful e-commerce store prioritizes clarity and simplicity. Shoppers should be able to quickly locate products through intuitive navigation, well-structured categories, and effective filtering options. A homepage or landing page should immediately communicate your brand's value proposition, providing strong calls-to-action (CTAs) that encourage visitors to explore further or make a purchase. Product pages should be compelling and informative, featuring high-quality images, detailed descriptions, and social proof such as customer reviews to build confidence.

Optimizing Performance And Accessibility

Speed and accessibility play critical roles in user experience. A slow-loading website frustrates visitors and leads to higher bounce rates, meaning fewer conversions. Optimizing site speed through image compression, streamlined coding, and limiting third-party scripts ensures a faster, smoother browsing experience.

Accessibility should never be an afterthought. Making your store readable, navigable, and usable for all customers improves the shopping experience for everyone. Ensuring proper color contrast, scalable font sizes, keyboard-friendly navigation, and screen reader compatibility expands your audience and demonstrates inclusivity. Accessibility isn't just a compliance checkbox – it's a way to make sure every potential customer can shop comfortably.

Using Apps And Plugins Wisely

Third-party apps can greatly enhance functionality, but they should be added with intention. Many store owners make the mistake of installing too many plugins, leading to performance slowdowns and unnecessary complexity. Instead, apps should be carefully chosen based on their direct impact on user experience, business goals, and operational efficiency.

Conducting regular plugin audits and removing unnecessary apps ensures your site remains fast and efficient. If multiple apps provide overlapping features, consolidating them into a single, well-rounded solution can improve both performance and manageability.

How to Audit and Improve Your Site

E-commerce success requires ongoing optimization, not just a one-time setup. Regularly auditing your website helps identify areas for improvement and ensures that your store remains competitive. A thorough website audit includes evaluating site speed, mobile responsiveness, SEO performance, and conversion rates.

Site speed is one of the most important factors influencing user experience and search rankings. Tools like Google PageSpeed Insights or GTmetrix provide insights into load times and pinpoint optimization opportunities. If performance issues arise, reducing image file sizes, eliminating unnecessary scripts, and enabling browser caching can dramatically improve efficiency.

Usability testing is another crucial aspect of optimization. I always recommend store owners browse their site as if they were a customer, testing navigation, product search, and the checkout process. Are there any broken links? Do menus make sense? Are any steps confusing? Conducting A/B tests on landing pages, product descriptions, and CTA buttons can provide valuable data on what resonates best with customers and what needs improvement.

SEO performance should be monitored consistently using Google Search Console and analytics tools. Product pages should be optimized with the right keywords and meta descriptions, and tracking metrics like bounce rate and session duration can reveal whether visitors are finding the information they need or leaving too soon. If engagement metrics are low, consider updating product descriptions, improving site navigation, or adding more engaging content.

Accessibility checks should also be part of your audit process. Automated tools like WAVE or AXE can help identify accessibility issues, but real-user testing is just as important. Making sure that text is readable, navigation is intuitive, and screen readers can properly interpret content ensures your store is usable by all customers, not just those without disabilities.

When to Hire a Professional

Designer or Consultant

While many store owners successfully manage their website design and maintenance, there are times when bringing in a professional can make all the difference. A skilled designer or e-commerce consultant can help you optimize user experience, improve site performance, and ensure that your store is positioned for long-term growth.

If your store is experiencing high bounce rates or low conversions, it may indicate that customers are struggling to navigate or engage with your site. A professional can analyze these issues and suggest solutions to improve user flow and increase conversions.

A complete website redesign is another instance where hiring an expert is beneficial. If your store feels outdated or doesn't align with your brand's image, working with a designer can modernize your site while ensuring it remains fast, responsive, and optimized for search engines.

For those needing custom functionality beyond what pre-built SaaS themes and plugins offer, a developer can create tailored solutions that integrate seamlessly with your platform. This is particularly useful if you require advanced automation, multi-channel selling integrations, or unique design elements that set your store apart from competitors.

Even if you've optimized your store on your own, persistent speed issues can signal a need for deeper technical adjustments. A consultant can conduct a thorough performance audit, identifying server-side bottlenecks, excess code, or inefficient scripts that may be slowing down your store.

Lastly, if your business is expanding into new markets or scaling rapidly, an expert can help you implement advanced e-commerce features, automate processes, and streamline operations to handle higher order volumes efficiently.

Bringing in a professional doesn't mean you have to give up control over your store. Instead, it allows you to focus on growing your business while ensuring that your website is fully optimized, functional, and ready to support your long-term success.

Final Thoughts

The most successful e-commerce websites strike the right balance between design, usability, and performance. Every design choice should be made with the customer's journey in mind, from the moment they land on the site to the completion of their purchase. By applying the best practices outlined in this book – prioritizing intuitive navigation, streamlining checkout, improving site speed, ensuring accessibility, and strategically using third-party tools – you'll set your store up for long-term success.

Building a high-converting online store isn't about the perfect launch – it's about constant refinement and improvement. Regularly testing, analyzing performance, and listening to customer feedback will help you fine-tune your store to meet evolving expectations and industry trends. The goal isn't just to attract visitors, but to turn them into loyal customers who keep coming back.

With a thoughtful approach to web design, you can create a store that not only looks great but also functions seamlessly, helping you grow your business and stay ahead in the competitive world of e-commerce.

ABOUT THE AUTHOR

Danielle Mead

Danielle Mead is an e-commerce expert with over 25 years of experience working at dotcom startups and as an independent web designer and consultant. She has worked with over 600 clients across industries to launch and optimize online stores that deliver results. Her one-woman company, Duck Soup E-Commerce, primarily works with clients on the BigCommerce platform, empowering online retailers with practical tools and strategies to overcome challenges and succeed in competitive markets. She is passionate about simplifying the complexities of e-commerce and creating clear, actionable plans for success. Learn more about Danielle and her services at her website https://ducksoupecommerce.com.